THIS BOOK FOUND YOU!

THIS BOOK FOUND YOU!

So Pick It Up and Read It

BERONICA PARHAM

gatekeeper press
Columbus, Ohio

The views and opinions expressed in this book are solely those of the author and do not reflect the views or opinions of Gatekeeper Press. Gatekeeper Press is not to be held responsible for and expressly disclaims responsibility of the content herein.

THIS BOOK FOUND YOU!
So Pick It Up and Read It

Published by Gatekeeper Press
2167 Stringtown Rd, Suite 109
Columbus, OH 43123-2989
www.GatekeeperPress.com

Copyright © 2022 by Beronica Parham

All rights reserved. Neither this book, nor any parts within it may be sold or reproduced in any form or by any electronic or mechanical means, including information storage and retrieval systems, without permission in writing from the author. The only exception is by a reviewer, who may quote short excerpts in a review.

Library of Congress Control Number: 2022940274

ISBN (paperback): 9781662927072
eISBN: 9781662927089

Contents

INTRODUCTION	3
1. POSITIVE THINKING	**9**

Positive Thoughts
How to Maintain Positive Thoughts
The Benefits of a Positive Mindset
Belief in a Higher Power

2. THE POWER OF SUBCONSCIOUS THOUGHTS	**19**

Train Your Subconscious Mind
How Subconscious Thoughts Influence Life

3. VIBRATIONS	**35**

What Are Vibrations?
How to Raise Your Emotional State

4. THE ACT OF FORGIVENESS	**45**
5. THE LAW OF ATTRACTION	**51**

Vibrations
Like Attracts Like
Our Thoughts Affect Us Physically

6. GRATITUDE	**59**

How Gratitude Helps Attract What You Want
How Do You Express Gratitude?
Gratitude Even in Times of Despair
Gratitude As a Practice

FINAL THOUGHTS	73
ACKNOWLEDGEMENTS	77
REFERENCES	79

This Book Found You!
INTRODUCTION
...

You found this book for a reason.

There is something within these pages that you need to know at this moment—be it a new idea, or a reawakening of something you learned long ago. All too often, many of us remain in our comfort zone and stay complacent, accepting where we are in this moment, and we do not dare to rock the boat. We accept without question what happens in our lives, both the good and bad, as just life. We may dream about what could be or what something could become. But we do not take any action to move forward.

Does this sound familiar? This is why **This Book Found You**. For many years, I lived my life by society's rules and believed that I needed to do what everyone else deemed appropriate to be successful and happy. I followed society's blueprint: went to school, graduated from college, had multiple jobs, got married, had children, and struggled financially at times. Trying to live up to other people's expectations, I based my happiness on how I appeared to others and what they thought of me. I gave away my power, not even realizing I had any. As a result, I constantly felt the pressure to be better than I was and do better than I did.

Have you decided to just accept where you are in your life? Are you feeling some of the same pressures that I did? I believe so because **This Book Found You!** To others, my life appeared great. There were no

INTRODUCTION

real complaints. My work was fine, and my family was healthy. However, I was never truly happy. I had this nagging feeling that something was missing and that I was not living the life that I was meant to live. I knew that I was destined for so much more. When I expressed my concerns to others, I received comments such as, "You are already doing fine. Why would you want more?" I tried to make sense of these external comments and be ok with where I was, but my efforts never lasted. I still did not feel whole and knew that there had to be more to life than what I was experiencing.

My desire to learn how *not* to let other people's limiting beliefs become my reality and how to create the life I truly wanted, put me on the journey to find some answers. I have had the privilege of studying with someone who helped me to see that all these things I wanted were possible and were in my reach to achieve. It was an awakening. Starting my spiritual journey allowed me to realize that I was capable, worthy, and not alone. When we can be completely honest and truthful with ourselves there is freedom in the knowing.

I have studied, researched, and learned the process of goal setting, eliminating limiting beliefs, planning for change, and implementing that change. As I studied and expanded spiritually, I could see my life changing. I began to see more positive change in myself. Inner peace and understanding were coming into my consciousness. I started to see things differently and became more compassionate and fearless. I realized that I do have the power to change things in my life. I finally listened to myself and set boundaries. By doing these things, I gradually began to feel whole.

The first time I noticed things were changing for me was when I realized I was not as angry as I had been. I started to see people and situations differently. I began to understand that it was my perception and acceptance of the pain and/or wrongdoing that was causing me to hold on to the resentment and anger. Can you imagine the freedom that you have when you know that you do not have to take on other people's problems? My thoughts and feelings about people whose names would trigger feelings of anger and rage in me from past experiences became just a memory with no emotional attachment. I was not holding on to past hurts anymore. I was changing, and they no longer had power over me. To be able to truly forgive and understand that when people lash out and do hurtful things, it was not about me, and **I did not have to accept it**—this was big for me.

The results of my journey so far has been a spiritual release and renewal. Using the tools described in this book, I have become more aware of who I truly am, and with this understanding, I have been able to focus on what is best for me. Does that mean that I no longer have feelings of anger, sadness, fear, or uncertainty? Of course not, but I do have the tools to get myself back on track faster and get back into a place of love, hope, gratitude, and joy.

I have seen remarkable change not only in myself but in others who started to approach their lives with an unlimited mindset. It didn't take long for people to notice a positive shift. When I started coaching, the comment I remember most was, "I thought it would take forever for me to see any change. I am surprised at how quickly this shift has happened."

This improvement is what I want for all of us. Therefore, I felt it was necessary to share what I have learned and how to achieve whatever you may want by changing the way you think. *This Book Found You* is a product of what I have learned by using tools to help in the change that I was seeking. I take people on a journey that visits the six key ideas to help them live happier, more fulfilling lives. They include the following:

INTRODUCTION

1. Positive Thinking
2. Controlling the Subconscious Mind
3. Understanding Vibrations
4. Forgiveness
5. The Law of Attraction
6. Gratitude

You might start to wonder how you can get things done and really move things from being just a thought to reality. You act and move one step at a time. Each chapter of this book contains practical recommendations you can implement in your daily life.

When you begin to transform your thinking, accept the possibility for change, and become aligned with your spiritual self, you can surrender and create the life you want to live. Of course, thoughts need to be followed by actions. If you take no action, then nothing changes, and thoughts remain just ideas and dreams.

> *"We are responsible for what we are, and whatever we wish ourselves to be, we have the power to make ourselves".*
> —SWAMI VIVEKANANDA

What you will discover in the following pages has the potential to completely change your life. When push comes to shove, you are ultimately and entirely responsible for your thoughts, actions, and successes in life. You will gain insight through practicing and opening your mind to potentially new ideas, or you may be revisiting these topics to make the commitment to implement them into your daily life. Make these a daily practice and watch how your life improves. Are you ready for the transformation? Yes, you are because **This Book Found You!** It is your life; you can do this and see minimal or dramatic positive change—it is up to you.

> *"You are the conductor of your own attitude! Nobody else can compose your thoughts for you".*
> —LEE J. COLAN

Chapter One
POSITIVE THINKING

...

Positive thinking isn't about ignoring the negative or trying to wish it away with positive thoughts. It is about seeing the obstacle for what it is and being positive that you'll have the strength to get through it.

> *"The mind is everything. What you think, you become".*
> —BUDDHA

Positive Thoughts

Did you know that right now, you are a perfect expression of infinite power? There is nothing that is impossible; everything that you want can be a reality for you. As you become more aware of your connection with the infinite power within you, that awareness will be reflected in everything you do and achieve.

Changing the way you think and becoming aware of who you truly are takes time; it is a process. It requires replacing old negative/bad habits, and conditioning with more positive thoughts that will lead to

1 » POSITIVE THINKING

more positive behavior. Most likely, you were conditioned with all types of ideas and so-called truths, which have become fixed in your subconscious mind. Today, they could be causing you grief, preventing you from achieving the things you want in your life. These limitations are holding you back from moving forward. These ideas, truths, and thoughts that became your habitual way of looking at the world cause the unwanted results you are currently getting. The more you practice positive thinking, the easier it becomes to break these old habits and form a new way of thinking.

Positive thinking does not mean that you begin to ignore the unpleasantries in life, but it does mean that you can approach difficult situations from a different perspective. Positive thinking isn't about ignoring the negative or trying to wish it away with positive thoughts. It is about seeing the obstacle for what it is and being *positive* that you'll have the strength to get through it.

A person who practices positive thinking can shift those all-consuming negative thoughts and start focusing on something positive much faster. Learning to stay in a positive state by being aware of what you are thinking, doing, and feeling is necessary to thrive and grow. Do you find yourself looking for outside influences to make you happy? If so, you have to begin to look within yourself instead. Happiness is something that is inside every one of us—it is not external. When you are focused on the negative aspects of your life, they may often cause stress or anxiety and ruin your day. But when you have a positive mindset and stay in a state of gratitude and appreciation, you will likely find yourself smiling more often, being friendly to strangers, and becoming more understanding and compassionate.

Are you able to focus on positive emotions? Can you imagine feeling hope, love, courage, confidence, and joy? Can you feel the strength that comes with these emotions? What is the worst thing that can happen to you if you are hopeful, joyful, or confident?

If you felt courage and confidence, what would you do? Would this move you to take action and move toward the things you really want?

I want you to breathe and open up to invite these positive feelings into your life. Can you start to think positive and imagine living a life of joy and gratitude? The very first step is to start to see yourself living the life you want and to see what is possible. When you can feel joy, hope, love, courage, and gratitude for yourself, you can start to take the steps needed that will help you let go of whatever may be holding you back and create the life that you truly want.

Emotions and thoughts impact every aspect of our lives. Sometimes it feels like our emotions just totally consume us. So how do we get our emotions under control, so they no longer impact us and control our lives? We take our Power Back!

I was never taught that I could control my thinking or had the capability of releasing negative thoughts, but now I have found that we have the ability to do so. We first need to acknowledge what we are feeling. There is a place for all of our emotions; there is a place for anger, resentment, sadness, fear, and anxiety.

To acknowledge how you feel, you can find a quiet place, close your eyes, take a few deep breaths, and say to yourself or out loud:

I am feeling _____ (what emotion you are feeling).
This is why I am feeling _____ (emotion you are feeling).
Even though I am feeling _____ (emotion you are feeling),
I can still accept the way I feel, love myself, and move forward.

This structure allows you to pinpoint what you are feeling and why, but also to understand that it is OK to feel what you are feeling. Notice

1 » POSITIVE THINKING

what comes up and write it down. When you are still and open, you can hear the message that is meant for you. Listen to yourself and your body.

> *"If you want to clean house, you first have to see the dirt".*
> —LOUISE HAY

Most importantly, do not beat yourself up about how you feel. Just acknowledge your feelings. The ability to be compassionate with yourself and all your feelings will help you start to heal. If you are open to making a positive change, then you can begin the journey. Once you realize that you do have power over what you are thinking and understand that YOU ARE ENOUGH, you can start to shift yourself into the true powerful you.

It was over three years ago when I started to focus on the practice of positive thinking and having a positive mindset. By changing my perception of the world around me, I quickly saw changes in the world and in myself. I did pray for strength and freedom from what was weighing heavy on my mind, but it became much more profound work than that. I found that when one is in a more positive state, more positive things tend to show up. When we can start to think and focus on more positive thoughts, we begin to expect good to come, and guess what? Good things will come.

When we intentionally focus on positive thoughts, our actions will be such that our connection with our feelings and our interactions with others will positively improve our overall well-being. When I am feeling overwhelmed or upset and just feeling low, I just do what comes naturally and breathe. I direct my mind to the truth of higher consciousness by finding a peaceful place and becoming quiet. Then I close my eyes and just breathe. I take deep breaths and exhale slowly until I start to feel better. I breathe in through my nose and breathe out through my mouth. It's incredibly relaxing. Once I get to a place where I feel like I'm grounded and calm, I move forward with affirmations, intentions, or prayer. Mindful breathing is my tool for grounding myself, getting in the correct mindset, and becoming clear so that I can refocus my attention on something more positive that will help me with whatever negative emotions I am experiencing.

In my life, I have received so much good: good in relationships, good in financial abundance, and good health. When good things happened to you, do you remember how you were feeling? What were you thinking? Having a positive mindset allows you to attract more good. This does not stop negative things from happening, but it gives me the help needed to change my thoughts, which helps to change my perception. Before I became mindful of how I perceived the world, I was going through my life on autopilot and living in a reactive state. I wasn't a mess—not outwardly, at least; I was still able to meet goals and be successful, but often, everything was more complicated than it needed to be. That all started to change when I was able to see things in a more positive light. Once I shifted my mindset, I started to expect good things to happen for me, and with that, I opened myself up to see opportunities and possibilities that were obscured before. Simply put, when I started to expect good things, good things came.

When we come into this life, I believe we have a path and a purpose. Most of us spend most of our lives trying to figure out what that path is. I still often check inwardly and ask if I am on the right path, and I find the answers become more accessible if I ask with the right intention. In my opinion, we made an agreement, or pact, before we came into this human existence to take a particular route throughout our life, full of trials and tribulations but also packed with hidden Easter eggs of oppor-

1 » POSITIVE THINKING

tunity. Once we can truly be open and start to expect good things for ourselves, these hidden Easter eggs will begin to line up for us. Multiple opportunities will start to show up. The truth is they were always there, but until we expect good things to happen, we are unable to see or even imagine what is possible.

How to Maintain Positive Thoughts

Although it is impossible to avoid adversity altogether, individuals who have a positive attitude will always bounce back quickly. Consciously, you can only focus on one thought at a time. So, when you notice a negative thought, you can replace it with a more positive one. It is not about denying that there are difficulties in life that bring negative feelings or negative thoughts with them, but rather about changing how you respond to an event using carefully selected words, thoughts, or ideas that can transform your outlook.

For example, instead of referring to a problem as a problem, call it a situation, puzzle, or challenge. The rephrasing of a single word will help you interpret the event more objectively and change your perspective to see things from a different view, thus changing your narrative. For example, instead of saying, "I have a problem," consider saying, "I have been introduced to a new challenge, or situation, or even a surprise opportunity."

The Benefits of a Positive Mindset

By making positive thinking a habit and consistently retraining your brain, you will naturally develop a positive mindset and gain many benefits, including gratitude, integrity, flexibility, optimism, and resilience. Along with a positive mindset, you will find it possible to calmly accept less-desirable situations, see things from another perspective, and begin to see the lessons and growth potential within them. When you are in a state of gratitude, you will be able to accept what comes and find the reason to be grateful even in bad times.

Science and spiritual practices prove that positive thinking provides real value in our lives. Focusing on and practicing positive thinking can rewire your brain and enhance positive feelings. Like anything, to become a master, we must practice; we have to work at it. Think about exercising; we must perform the exercises to achieve the desired results. Dr. Barbara L. Fredrickson is the Kenan Distinguished Professor at the University of North Carolina and author of the book *Positivity*, which provides excellent insight into positive thinking and its impact on our lives. Dr. Fredrickson states in her book, "When your soul is stirred by the sheer beauty of existence; or when you feel energized and excited by a new idea, or hobby, positivity reigns whenever positive emotions—like love, joy, gratitude, serenity, interest, and inspiration—touch and open your heart" (Fredrickson, 2009).

As we continue to explore all the good things that happen when we begin to think positive, it's important to remember that there is a place for negative thoughts or bad feelings. When I talk about negative thinking, I am not talking about negativity. There is a difference. "Negativity" means having a bad attitude. Negativity is seen in someone who is always angry, cynical, and complaining about being helpless or sad all of the time regardless of the situation. "Negative thinking" is having the ability to see or feel the dark side of people, ideas, places, and things that allows us to respond to them in order to protect ourselves. They are necessary and crucial to our experience. Negative emotions enable us to sharpen our awareness in the wake of danger; this is essential to our survival. Negative feelings could help you set boundaries; it can help you to be cautious when making decisions. If you experience negative emotions, give yourself some time to investigate them and see if they are part of negativity or just negative thinking.

Belief in a Higher Power

When some of us think about a higher power we may think of a deity or supernatural being. Some of us believe it is a supreme being that is greater than other gods. For some, it is a single, all-knowing God or a conception of the power of a God. Then there are people who don't believe in beings. They believe the universe or nature itself is a higher power. Some people believe group consciousness is a higher power.

Believing in a higher power can help us find purpose. It does not matter the name you give this higher power, or if you name it at all, but when you have faith in something bigger than yourself you can find peace. The idea of a higher power is simple—it is a connection. People need and want to feel connected to something. Knowing that we have a place in this world and knowing we aren't alone will give us strength.

It is human nature for us to want to feel a part of something and to have that feeling of belonging. Most people don't choose a higher power. They go through a spiritual process and subconsciously connect with a higher power. As they grow to understand that power, the connection grows in their consciousness. They experience a spiritual awakening and realize the connection exists. It is often disputed which practices are the most valid—whether they are spiritual or scientific—but I suggest that both are valid routes to positivity.

Shamans, for example, perform certain rituals to get in touch with their higher power and use certain medicines and drugs to help them reach higher realms. I don't personally use any substances to get to that place, but there is no judgement here. If it helps others, I respect it. I wouldn't criticize anybody's practices to find a connection with a higher source.

In paganism, the concept is that they give back to their ancestors. Often during either a full moon or new moon, they go on a pilgrimage and offer a gift to their ancestors. It's said that pagans often receive visions and messages from ancestors to help them on their journey. I like the concept of recognizing our ancestors because I do believe that they are here supporting us.

I like to take time to understand and explore other ideas, philosophies, and practices from many different cultures, as each individual will resonate differently with different practices. It's a journey toward oneself.

One of the best ways to start to change your current state is with positive thinking. Having a positive mindset will change your life! Understanding that negative or bad things will still happen but remembering to breathe through the tough moments, believing in a higher power, and shifting your focus to a more positive thought as quickly as you can gives you the strength to overcome obstacles and achieve your goals.

As we leave this chapter, I believe this quote from Henry Ford sums it up: "If you think you can or think you can't, you are right." It is easy to let your thinking run amuck for all the things you want in your life, but when you practice being intentional with your thoughts and focus more on the good, you are able to see opportunities that will lead you on the path to obtaining your goals.

Chapter Two

THE POWER OF SUBCONSCIOUS THOUGHTS

...

*The conscious mind is the camera,
and the subconscious is the image. Point your camera
only at the things you want to capture.*

The power of the subconscious mind is insurmountable, and once you learn to use that power to your advantage, you can attain new opportunities for success and happiness. To begin harnessing this power, you must first understand the differences between the subconscious mind and the conscious mind.

The conscious mind is that "in the moment" awareness. It encompasses your current thoughts, physical well-being, and the emotions that you extract from your immediate environment. The subconscious mind acts as a storage system for all thoughts, memories, beliefs, skills, and past experiences. It serves as an innate guidance system that monitors life occurrences and dictates your response to them.

There are a few metaphors that I find helpful when thinking about the difference between the conscious and subconscious mind. The first metaphor is that the conscious mind selects and plants seeds, and the

2 » THE POWER OF SUBCONSCIOUS THOUGHTS

subconscious germinates and grows them—make sure you choose the best seeds you want to harvest. Your conscious mind is in the here and now. It is in this very moment: what you're seeing, what you're dealing with, and what you're doing right now. The subconscious mind records your thoughts and actions. When you think and act in a specific way, you plant certain seeds. So be mindful and careful about what you are thinking and what you are doing so that you know you are exhibiting thoughts and behavior worthy of the beautiful garden that you wish to grow. Choose your thoughts carefully. Look for the thoughts that bring you peace, love, and joy.

It is so important to be aware of your thoughts and actions. When we react to things without thinking, we leave ourselves open to forming negative thought patterns, and it can all become unraveled very quickly. For every action, there's a reaction, and it can create a long-term effect of positive or negative subconscious thinking depending on how we act in the conscious moment.

Here is another metaphor I like. The conscious mind is the camera, and the subconscious is the image. Point your camera only at the things you want to capture. You may question how you point the camera away from lousy input? How do you shut out any negativity?

For me, it's all about perception. I have a tree outside my house that I look to for strength. You could argue that it's just a tree (which is how I used to view it), but now I have made a conscious decision to see it as a pillar of strength. When I focus on that tree, I have a true respect for nature. I can see the beauty, strength, and support in its image. I point my lens at this tree and it somehow grounds and heals me. I've looked at my tree for twenty years now, but it was only when I started to change the way I was thinking did my perception change. I began to understand that in order to stay more positive, I had to look for the good in everything.

You can always find something more positive to focus on, even if it is a small something. When you are able to change your perception to see more good, things begin to look different, and there is a positive shift that happens. Reaching an awareness that our conscious mind is here and now, I find it incredibly important to remember that my behavior and how I perceive people, places, and things will affect how I feel and interact with everything around me in every moment. If your conscious mind is a camera, you are the photographer. You are in control. You decide where you point your camera. Point your camera only at the things you want to capture. Being in a positive state of mind, you can create a better image for yourself.

Train Your Subconscious Mind

It is essential to be aware of our thoughts, so we can choose the most positive and good feeling possible in the moment. This awareness and choice is something that we have to practice. Regardless of what habits, beliefs, and thought patterns you have developed throughout your life, it is possible to create new ones by training your subconscious mind.

As I mentioned earlier, what you give your attention to equates to what you are asking for, whether it's genuinely what you want or not. The energy of your thoughts, negative or positive, wanted or unwanted, is your request to the Universe, to God, to Source, or to whomever you are asking.

The following steps can improve that perpetual communication between the conscious and subconscious by training the subconscious mind to predominately serve as your ally, guiding you toward your goals and dreams.

2 » THE POWER OF SUBCONSCIOUS THOUGHTS

1. Limit Exposure to Negativity

Let's investigate this idea more deeply. The subconscious mind absorbs information and forms beliefs based on all the minute details of your daily interactions, encounters, and environment. So, the first step toward training your subconscious mind is to limit the amount of negativity you're exposed to. This includes people, social media, television, and so on. As often as possible, find opportunities to surround yourself with optimistic, happy people; read and watch positive, inspiring things. Eventually, positive feelings and aspirations will replace fear.

When I was younger, I used to enjoy watching horror films and gore movies. It seems odd to me now, but that's what I used to watch all the time. I'm not sure what part of my psyche was interested in such input, but as I wasn't conscious of limiting negative information, I allowed it into my life. I was engulfed in it, and it affected me, even though I was unaware of it at the time. Hindsight is 20/20, and looking back, I see my younger self complaining and generally unhappy. It started to affect me so negatively that I began having bad dreams and unwanted visions; that was the consequence.

This negative input changed the way I saw people. I was getting paranoid, judging everyone, only able to see the negative aspects of their personality. I became that person who would cross the street to avoid any possible interaction with strangers. Now there are times when it may be necessary to cross the street, but I am more aware of the actions I take and why. Making small changes to media inputs allowed me to be more joyous and happier versus fearful and distrusting. I now read more and watch animated films, comedies, or educational documentaries. Limiting negativity is not a matter of dumbing down your interests; rather, it allows you to sidestep into positivity.

2. Visualize

The subconscious mind responds well to images, so practice visualization for a few minutes a day and focus on what you want in life. Try visualizing that dream home or ideal vacation. Imagine what the perfect relationship or career looks and feels like. Make sure you include every bit of detail you want, incorporating not only visual images in your mind but the feelings of joy, pride, and satisfaction that would come with making it your reality.

There are several different tools you can use: you could use a dream board or use the written word by journaling, especially when the words are your own. If it comes from you, it will come back to you.

I've been working on manifesting something that will be life-changing for my family. Since this is the first time that we are talking about manifesting, let me give you a definition. On the spiritual level, manifestation is simply bringing that which we cannot see into existence. It is believed that thoughts have an energy of their own, which attracts whatever the person is thinking. This energy itself is neither positive nor negative—it simply is.

The one very important fact that I have learned is that you must be clear on what you want. Getting a clear vision may take a while; you might have to ask yourself the question "What do I really want?" over and over again until you know what you truly want. When I started working on the process of manifestation, it took me over a year just to get a clear vision of what I really wanted. At first, I thought I knew exactly what I wanted. But then, as I dug deeper, I began to understand that what I wanted could show up in many ways. So, I had to narrow my focus and think, "If this is truly what I want, what are all the aspects that make up what I want?" To keep my vision clear, I started to gather pictures of things that I believed were the most important to me. As I looked at pictures and thought about what I really wanted, that vision began to change over time.

To help keep my eye on the prize, I made a vision board with pictures, quotes, and affirmations. This process allowed me to stay focused. I look at my board every day and have it strategically placed, so it is the first thing I see every morning. It gives me inspiration. As I continue to work on my vision, I may add to my board or, in some cases, start a new one.

Once I had that clear picture, I started to see aspects of what I wanted to manifest in meditation. The vision did not come all at once, but in parts. This let me know that the work was being done, and I just needed to be patient. Being patient did not mean that I did not have to take actions that would move me closer to obtaining what I wanted, but I knew that something greater than me was working out how it would come.

I also found that it's a process, and you should try and enjoy each moment as the process unfolds. Once I started to enjoy the process, I experienced feelings of joy and excitement.

What I described is my approach to visualization. I know other people have different takes on it. Some people say, "Ask, see it, feel it, and it's going to come."

I like that, but instead, I would say, "Ask, visualize, feel it, *take action*, and surrender. Then it will come." You must take action toward achieving what you want. When you have a clear vision and are open to seeing opportunities, it will lead you to the right actions to take to achieve your goal.

3. Practice Positive Self-Talk and Affirmations

We experience a lot of internal dialogue. We talk to ourselves all day, every day, and the way we do it makes a huge difference in our lives. Negative thoughts and feelings may be bombarding you, but if you can change your focus and just move one step closer to a more positive thought, you will feel better. When you start to alter those conversations with yourself, you will start to shift your subconscious—in a sense, retrain your brain. One way to help with the internal self-talk is to consider spending time each day repeating affirmations.

Affirmations make the most significant impact when you create simple, straightforward, unambiguous statements that focus on the present tense and align with what you want and believe. Here are a few examples of affirmations that you may use to help you align with what you truly want and believe:

- I am successful and so excited to experience the financial abundance that I know I deserve.
- I am grateful for everything that I have.
- I am worthy.
- I am Divine Love.
- I am confident.
- I am patient.

How do you go about implementing these things into your daily life?

When I wake up in the morning, I always say, "Today's going to be a great day." I may go into a little bit more detail and add the things that are going to make it a great day.

I say my affirmations out loud, as it piques my emotions and vibrations, but you can also say them in your head. The main thing is, once you are clear about your affirmation, you repeat the same thing over and over. I typically try to say it at least three times, but you can do it as long as you feel necessary. *It's totally up to you, as it's coming from within you.* Affirmations are an emotional thing and mean different things to different people.

Can you stand in front of a mirror and say, "I am beautiful, and I am wonderful!" or does it make you uncomfortable? To be clear in what you want, you have to believe it. I have been working on this process every day for some time now, and I know and believe that I am a true expression of God, and I am worthy of everything that I want in my life. In the beginning, it was difficult for me to accept, but as I continue to practice the tools that I discuss in this book, I have gained an awareness, commitment, and belief that I have never had before. If you're new to this concept, try saying your affirmations in the mirror. This will help you as you become more comfortable in the belief that you are worthy of what you want. You must decide what works for you; whether it needs to be shouted into the sky, or whispered into your pillow, then so be it. Follow your heart. I know my neighbors probably wonder what the hell I am talking about when I am doing my affirmations, but that's okay—I'm passionate about it, and I'm over being embarrassed by it. I listen to myself, and how I affirm all depends on how I feel.

Affirmations make the most significant impact when you create simple, straightforward, unambiguous statements. Talk about things in the present tense. Rather than saying, "I want this to be my life," say, "This is already in my life."

Know and trust that you deserve it.

4. Do Not Let Fear or Doubt Interfere

In our society, we are taught to care what others think so much, so we look to others for approval and support. While it is certainly good to have a support system, you should never allow others' opinions to cast shadows of doubt on what you want or know you can achieve.

THIS BOOK FOUND YOU

> *"What other people think of you is not your business. If you start to make that business your business, you will be offended for the rest of your life".*
>
> —DEEPAK CHOPRA

Have you ever been excited about something, like a new idea, and then shared that information with someone you perceived as a friend or a close family member? Then the first thing that came out of their mouth was not the support you were expecting. Instead, you heard, "Are you sure you should be wanting or planning to do that?"

They immediately started to cast negativity and doubt onto you. What if the real issue is that they are expressing concern because they might not want you to get too excited, over the top, or become disappointed? Could they be casting their own limiting beliefs that have nothing to do with you? So, one of the things that I've learned is not to share my ideas with anybody while they are half-baked.

I consciously stopped those conversations because it was causing me to rethink my ideas and rethink what I'd worked so hard to figure out. Outside influences can be well-meaning, but they can set us back. Now, I choose not to say anything to anybody until I am ready and sure that their responses will not affect the outcome. In the meantime, I keep doing what I need to do in the background.

Most of the people don't mean any harm. For example, some folks will tell you that you're already doing well and expect you to be content with where you are. They wonder why you would want more. "You've got a good job; you've got a nice house. So, what's your problem? Why can't you be happy or content?" I appreciate their opinion, but I cannot let other people's limitations influence me.

You must be very careful when people speak to you in that way because you may begin to rethink. "Well, maybe I should be content where I'm at. Maybe my big dream isn't possible," and the self-doubt creeps in. Even though other people may trample on your ideas or dreams unintentionally, you must stop it if it's happening.

5. Acknowledge the Small Achievements

Sometimes you can get caught in the big picture and stay so focused on the end goal that you can become overwhelmed and discouraged. If you feel that way, you should look at the situation and ask yourself a question: "What is the absolute smallest one thing that I can do right now, at this moment, today, to move me toward my goal?"

It could be something minor, like having a conversation to understand your possibilities. It could be simply researching, making one call, writing one list, or completing one task. Once you do that one thing, you can then pivot and move to stay on the right path.

Putting your focus on your big goals is necessary but achieving them is possible only by taking incremental steps. Also, the small wins are significant because they help you grow and continue in the excitement and feeling of "This is achievable! I can do this!" To stay motivated as you continue to move toward your larger goal, take the time to acknowledge and celebrate your small wins along the way.

Think about people who are on a weight-loss journey, fitness journey, or trying to overcome addictions. If they say to themselves, "Today I will no longer use drugs, I will never have another drink, I am going to lose twenty pounds, etc." they could very well be successful. However, a slip could introduce feelings of failure that could become overwhelming and create feelings of doubt that could lead to giving up. So, when you are moving toward your big goals, try to remember that it is a journey. Take it one day at a time and do the best thing that you can do for that day. Each moment can be a victory that is moving you a little closer to your goal. With this attitude, it will be easier to say to yourself, "Okay, well, *today* I have been successful. I have power over what I do *today*." And then, if you can do that with everything, every day, it will keep your momentum going.

It's also important to remember that the bigger the goal, the longer it may take you to get there. If you stumble, do not be hard on yourself. Forgive yourself and try again. Remember, you are powerful! Work through the steps, and eventually, you will achieve your goal. Also, be mindful and ask yourself every day, "How am I doing today?" and be sure to listen to the answer. Remember to be flexible. Understand that if you're going down your path and you hit a roadblock, it means you may need to shift what you're doing and do something a little differently. It certainly doesn't mean giving up on your goal because you feel it is no longer attainable. You might need to do something a little different, that's all. The obstacles you may face along the way are powerful tools to let you know the areas that still may need to be worked out. Or they will provide more information on what you genuinely want or do not want.

6. Identify What's Holding You Back

When the subconscious thoughts prevent you from pursuing something you want, it is a sign of conflicting beliefs. This is the time to take inventory and allow yourself time to understand the underlying issues that could be causing the block.

I heard of a study that essentially stated that many people don't achieve their goal because when they see it in plain sight and see that it's attainable, they shy away from it out of fear—fear of potentially achieving something they've wanted so badly.

Many of the blockers I had were deeply rooted in beliefs I picked up when I was younger. I didn't want to outshine people because I didn't want to appear greedy or too ambitious. I didn't want to offend other people with my goals, as strange as that sounds. But now, those beliefs have changed, and I think, "I'm like a peacock. I am beautiful, and I want to be seen!"

I'm not concerned about what other people think anymore. I look at it from a different perspective; I consider that every success I have benefits not only myself but others. My success is not a hindrance; it's the opposite.

Every time we create or manifest something into our lives, we're adding to the bigger picture, and any time we grow as people, it helps us all grow.

So, identify what's holding you back. Do you need to have everything in place before you get started? This approach, in truth, means you will never get moving. If you want everything to be aligned and perfect before you move forward, you'll be waiting forever. Think hard. Does any of this sound familiar?

- **Perfectionism.** So many people have deep desires within themselves and truly want to achieve certain things in life. However, they will never move forward until everything is in place.
- **Failure.** Are you scared to fail? Failure is not to be feared. It is how we learn.
- **Excuses.** Enough said.

- **Procrastination.** Now is the best time to do what you want. Just do a little something today that will help you move forward and get closer to your goals.
- **Expectations.** Get rid of the scenarios in your head of how things should be and how people should act. Accept them as they are. Just keep doing what you know if it's right for you.
- **Distractions.** There are many pleasant, but time-wasting, activities that we may do throughout the day. Stay focused on what you want, enjoy the process, and limit those activities that only bring temporary happiness. True happiness is within your reach.

How Subconscious Thoughts Influence Life

Subconscious thoughts happen automatically, just as your heart beats and blood pumps. This part of the mind absorbs all the details in and around you, regardless of whether you notice it.

Think of the subconscious mind as having an autopilot feature that serves to protect you. It operates similarly to a computer that runs various preprogrammed functions. However, the autopilot can be very limiting. So, depending on what has been programmed into the subconscious mind, it may or may not serve you well.

When you learn to use it to your advantage, those subconscious thoughts can become powerful. Remember that your subconscious mind is a huge memory bank. It stores everything that you ever learned and experienced as well as how you responded to those events. The tricky part is that if you do not reprogram your subconscious, you will continue to respond to experiences the way you always have, keeping you in your comfort zone—a place that is familiar.

2 » THE POWER OF SUBCONSCIOUS THOUGHTS

Have you ever noticed that you feel a bit uncomfortable when you attempt to try something new? This is because your subconscious is not familiar with the new. It is familiar with what you already know. In order for you to grow, you have to get out of your comfort zone. You have to get comfortable with the uncomfortable.

So, whether you acknowledge your subconscious thoughts or not, they affect your life every day. Our thoughts and how we react to them are merely habits. Therefore, by learning to focus on more positive thoughts, your subconscious mind will eventually respond with new habits and patterns. Below are some ideas that may help you establish new habits:

- **See the *unchangeable really* change.** If you can see what seems to be impossible change, this is the first step in changing your program. Just be open to the possibility of change.
- **Don't let other people's fear make you question your success.** Other people will respond differently to your goals or successes based on where they are in their lives. If someone is happy and doing well, they may respond in a positive and supportive way. Others who may not be happy with their lives may respond to you with fear and doubt. The bottom line is, their responses have nothing to do with your success.
- **Don't worry *about the how*.** You need to be clear on what you want and not be consumed with how you think it will work out. Don't try to control every single step of the process. Life is full of surprises, so you have to be open to any possibility, even those that you may never have imagined.

THIS BOOK FOUND YOU

> *"Look closely at the present you are constructing; it should look like the future you are dreaming".*
> —ALICE WALKER

Using processes such as meditation, affirmations, visualization, and having a positive attitude will prove advantageous for you.

Chapter Three
VIBRATIONS
...

> *"Spirituality doesn't mean being happy all the time".*
>
> —NICOLE TUSTIN

What Are Vibrations?

Everything in the universe contains energy that vibrates on different frequencies, including solid objects, you, and me. According to Cassandra Sturdy, "We are a 'being' that is made up of different energy levels: physical, mental, emotional and spiritual. Each of these levels has a vibrational frequency, when combined to create your overall vibration of being."

> *"When you're low, you'll know. When you're high, you're in flow".*
>
> —MADISON GOLDBLECK

When I think about vibrations, I get both an emotional and a physical reaction. This makes sense—our emotions control where we are, how we feel, and the connection we have with others who are vibrating at

3 » VIBRATIONS

the same level. Emotions can be viewed as a location on a vibration scale where joy, love, freedom, forgiveness, gratitude, etc. are at the highest point, and doubt, worry, blame, jealousy, and fear are at the bottom end.

From my personal experience, I had to realize how important it is to stay at the higher registers of the vibrational scale. When you can raise your vibration, you can live a more positive and meaningful life. Do you want to be the best version of yourself? I believe we all want to be the best we can be.

When you make the commitment to live your best life, you will start to notice the things that are bringing you down. Could it be the people who you are spending time with? You have to let go of the things that no longer serve you. When you are aware of the negative energies that surround you, it is time to make a change. It is possible to live at the higher registers of the vibrational scale on a perpetual basis. However, it takes conscious work to do so. When you are truly aligned with the source of your higher power, there is a vibrational match. The key is to try and stay on the higher vibrational scale as long as possible.

When you make this change, you are ready to release the things of the past. Releasing past emotional hurts and resentments will allow you to release the lower vibrations and negative emotions, helping you raise your vibration and become a better you. We should always try to achieve our highest vibration through joy, love, freedom, gratitude, and appreciation. You can feel the vibration throughout your mind and body. When you're at your highest vibrational match, you are indeed in alignment. Think about a time when you were genuinely in a state of pure joy. You felt good, happy, and you knew that nothing could knock you down. You felt amazing, and that's where we want to stay if we can!

Below is an example of an
EMOTIONAL FREQUENCY SCALE,
which will help you determine
where you stand emotionally.

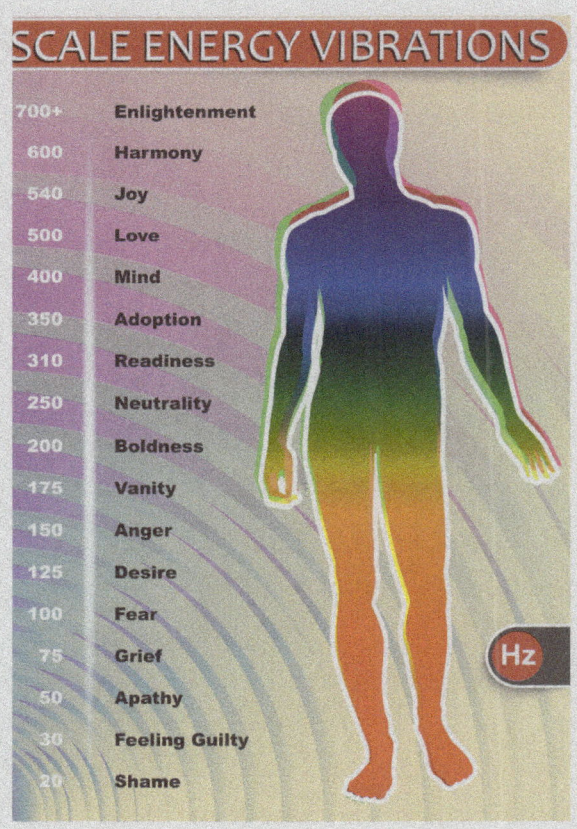

I want to emphasize that spirituality doesn't mean being happy all the time. We all experience times when our vibrations are on the lower registers, and these are the times when we need to be aware of our feelings and try to move to the next highest feeling. You can't simply jump from fear to joy. It just doesn't happen that way. But you can take baby steps up the vibrational ladder from shame, guilt, apathy, grief and fear to something that has a higher vibration, which could even be anger. Even though it is still a lower vibrational frequency, it may be higher on the vibrational scale than where you are in your present moment. Just try to continually get yourself to the best spot you can get to, step by step. You can think of them as lily pads on a pond—you can't jump across the pond in one leap. The higher the vibration, the better you will feel. Even though it's sometimes tempting to wallow in our own misery and to feed the beasts of fear and shame, it is simply an illusion to think that we are gaining anything from staying in these lower frequencies. Stepping toward a higher vibrational frequency is always the answer to a more positive self-awareness.

Once you are aware of what you are feeling in this very moment, you can determine if a shift to the next higher state is needed.

How to Raise Your Emotional State

Attempting to stay in the higher register is crucial. But how do we achieve this in our lives? The truth is, regardless of what you have been told or however many painful things you have experienced, you don't have to stay within the low registers for an extended period of time. There are many things that can help raise your vibration: smiling, saying "hello" to someone, or listening to music you enjoy. Even when you don't feel like smiling or stopping to admire a flower, try it and see how you feel afterward. I promise that when you start to become aware of your feelings, and you are able to move from the lower to the higher emotional frequencies, you will find greater joy in the smaller things.

Remember, we are focusing on raising our vibration in order to be in an excellent place to feel joy, love, appreciation, and empowerment. All these processes are to help you better understand where you are emotionally. As I've said, when you're in a better place, your vibration is higher, and you will attract those things that are a vibrational match. I have listed a few things that you can do to help shift your vibration to a higher level.

Gratitude

Gratitude is one of the quickest ways to raise your vibration. Take a minute and practice it now. Think about what you are thankful for right in this moment. It may be your family, the weather, your home, etc. Life coach Tony Robbins said, "You can't feel fear or anger while feeling gratitude at the same time." So, when you catch yourself at one of the lower frequencies, try thinking of something you are grateful for and see how your emotions shift.

Love

Can you think of someone who you love unconditionally? Visualize that they are with you right now. How do you feel? If you start to feel happiness or lightness, then this is the feeling you want, and your visualization is working to raise your vibration. Love is at the top of the vibration frequencies list, and it has the power to pull you up from the lower vibrational states. Focus on love, first and always.

Generosity

There is a saying that goes, "It is better to give than receive." Anytime you withhold from anyone or yourself, it lowers your vibration, and you feel bad. If you equate your happiness to something outside of yourself, it does not feel good. The fix is to be generous. Expressing generosity from a place of love, not obligation, will make you feel better. If you are feeling lonely? Try to make a stranger smile. Don't have enough time? Give your time to a good cause. Even donating a little money to a good cause will help to raise your vibration.

Forgiveness

When you cannot forgive, you carry with you feelings of anger, hostility, and stress. This will keep you in the lower registers of the vibrational scale, which can weigh on you so much that you may feel as if there is a ton of bricks on your back. If you are able to work toward forgiveness, you will release yourself of the lower energies and move up to feelings of empathy, compassion, and sympathy. This is truly a process (more on that later).

Positive Thinking

You become what you think about, and each thought you think creates your future. If the thoughts you think are pessimistic, overtly anxious, or in any way negative, you will likely find what you are looking for. Just as gratitude draws more of the same into your life, so does impatience, jealousy, and unworthiness. This negative energy can leave you feeling heavy and burdened. Be diligent about what thoughts you give your attention to.

Surround Yourself with Beauty

Make sure that your home and work environments reflect beauty, passion, and an enthusiasm for life. The right lighting can have a significant impact on your productivity and your mood. Hang art that inspires you. Use colors that calm and rejuvenate you. Reduce clutter and create more space for clarity. Your surroundings have a big effect on how you feel on the inside, and how you feel on the inside reflects outwardly.

I'm constantly trying to keep my vibration at the higher registers because if my vibration is high, it signifies that I am more in alignment with my true self, my source, or a higher power. When you are indeed in alignment and open to receiving, you start to see and feel things shift. You're more open to seeing new opportunities—you will start to have more positive experiences. When you are at a lower frequency, you only attract those things that are vibrating at the same frequency you are. Our vibrational frequency acts as a receiver for opportunities. Trying to stay within the higher registers is a service to yourself.

Meditation

Meditation is wonderful because it acts as a beautiful distraction from negative thoughts. It is a way to quiet the mind. If you're having a horrible day, try to meditate. It does not have to be long; ten to fifteen minutes will make a difference too. I know it can be hard to quiet your mind when you have so many thoughts coming at you, but don't give up! As with everything we have discussed, it is a process that takes practice. Stay with it and keep trying.

One weekend I drove with some relatives to Chicago, IL. We arrived safely and checked into our hotel. Even though I was tired, we went to meet up with my daughter and some other family members for dinner.

3 » VIBRATIONS

We had a lovely time, but I was utterly exhausted by the time I got back to the hotel room. I just wanted to get into bed. I got all comfy and began my meditation, and then five minutes in, the fire alarm went off.

I thought, "What the heck?"

I came out of the room and looked down the hall. I did not smell smoke but decided to go to the lobby to see what was going on. I met a gentleman in the lobby who told me that some kids were smoking marijuana in a room, and they had set off the smoke alarm.

The fire department came. They turned off the alarm, and I was like, "All right, fine. Now I'm going back to bed!"

By this time, it was around 1:30 am. I was exhausted by this point, but not wanting to give up, I got back into bed, took some deep breaths and was ready to start my meditation again. A few minutes into my meditation, the fire alarm went off again, although this time for only a few minutes. I didn't go downstairs, but I started to think that maybe I was just not supposed to meditate that night because every time I started, I was abruptly interrupted. I decided that instead of doing the meditation that night, I would pray. After my prayers, I set an intention to try meditation again in the morning.

So, I got up in the morning, and I did a morning meditation to start my day and just went on from there. I told you this story for two reasons: The first reason is so that you understand just how important mediation is for me. The second reason is that although I did my best to spend time in mediation that evening, it just did not work out. I did not beat myself up about it. I just accepted what was in that moment. Sometimes you can't focus because your brain will not calm down, and other times it's because of external forces that are impossible to drown out. Sometimes, the thoughts will keep coming. Even if you have done all the steps—breathing, focusing, settling down, etc.—you still cannot get there. Sometimes, I give myself a break, stop, and decide to come back later and try it again. I don't try to force it. Good vibrational energy is also about listening to what you want and need at any given time. It is constantly checking in with yourself.

Be Kind

When you give to someone else and do not expect anything in return, it feels good. This is because when you are helping someone else, you are not focused on a lack of anything. Your thinking is that of "I am grateful I have enough to share" or "I have more than enough to give to others." Do you recognize that abundance is a higher vibration? When you are thoughtful and kind to others, your vibration will rise. My grandmother was the pinnacle of selflessness. She may not have had a lot, but she gave to anyone who needed it. She did not focus on what she did not have but on the joy of helping others. So, you see, she was abundant.

In summation, try to be mindful of getting yourself to a higher vibration, step by step. Just focus on getting to the next highest register you can achieve, even if that is anger. Continue to climb to the next highest and then the next until you are vibrating at a frequency of love, gratitude, and appreciation. Remember, when your vibration is aligned with your higher power, all good things will come.

Chapter Four

THE ACT OF FORGIVENESS

...

There are some hurts you may never be able to forgive.

> *"To Forgive is to set a prisoner free and discover that the prisoner was you".*
>
> —LEWIS B. SMEDES

To forgive someone and to ask for forgiveness are the most important aspects of your spiritual growth. It is not just saying the words "I'm sorry," or "I forgive you." It is an emotion that is felt deep within you. When real forgiveness happens, there is a change that happens inside you. If you think you have forgiven someone, but there is no change in your emotions, then this lets you know there is still work to be done.

Forgiveness is necessary when you experience an event that has caused pain, hurt, or injury by someone else. Every one of us has the capacity to forgive, but when we are not able to forgive, it may be because our ego will not allow us to express forgiveness. By forgiving you are not **giving in but letting go** of that emotion that is so powerful that it seems to provide protection from the powerlessness that we feel when someone betrays us.

When we are angry, we invite the faults of others upon ourselves. ***Realize that when you forgive, you're not condoning another person's actions.*** Forgiveness is a personal decision to release someone from your condemnation. You're just letting yourself be free by forgiving them and accepting what happened. When you decide to forgive someone, it is not necessary to call them on the phone or approach them and tell them in person. You can forgive them from your heart, and they may never know. This is because forgiveness is not for them. It is for **YOU!**

We live in a society that appears to readily accept anger and resentment more than peace and forgiveness. Therefore, there are so many people that are not healed and suffer great emotional pain, and they act out because of that pain.

Forgiveness is something that I have been practicing daily. I started because I was so angry at so many for so long, that I was becoming a person I no longer recognized nor wanted to be. Some of these wrongs happened when I was a child, some as a teenager, and on through adulthood. I knew I had to do something because it was still causing me pain. I was so angry that just the thought of these people changed the way I felt, and I would become instantly enraged. Some of them had died and I was still angry.

So, I was told by someone very dear to me to do an exercise.

First you need to be grounded and clear. You do this by taking a few deep breaths and being still. Do this when and where you will not be disturbed and are able to be quiet.

Get a piece of paper. At the top of the paper write these words: "I fully release everything and everybody that is NOT part of my grand design of my LIFE. I forgive you. I bless you. I release you. I choose to live a life full of joy, love, and peace."

Then you start to write your list of people who you feel you need to forgive; this should include, but is not limited to, people who you may have caused harm in these areas of your life:

1. Your personal life
   ....
2. Family relationships
   ....
3. Career/job
   ....
4. Financial debt
   ....
5. Emotional (things that you want to be released from)
   ....
6. Situations you want to be released from

I was not initially surprised by the list of people that I wrote down. Then I flipped over the piece of paper, and I wrote a list of people who I felt needed to forgive me. Surprise, the list was very similar.

At the top of this paper, I wrote: "I release the past and allow myself to be forgiven. I will treat myself and others with respect and kindness moving forward."

So, I dug a little deeper, and one by one I really thought about what happened. I found that I played some part in just about every occurrence that I could remember.

Now this does not excuse or justify what was done, but it did provide me with an awareness of what happened and how it happened. We are responsible for ourselves and our behavior. We do not act out of revenge and hate even though at times we may feel justified. So, this exercise helped me to gain a new perspective, and I was able to forgive and release those feelings of hate and anger. This did **not** happen overnight. In some cases, it took years. But when I was truly able to forgive, it was if a weight were lifted.

Since I started this exercise, it has been like a door has been opened. I now remember situations with people that I'd completely forgotten about, or so I'd thought. At some of the strangest times, I will recall something or someone that needed to go on my list. I have been doing this for years now and my list is changing. There are things that have come off the list and things that have been added on.

This is ongoing, and at times I have to revisit some of the offenders on the list because the healing is not complete.

DISCLAIMER: There are some hurts you may never be able to forgive.

You may have wounds from your life or from when you were vulnerable that go deep. There are wounds that came because you had no control. This could be where someone you loved was injured, and you just can't see how you can ever fully forgive. The hurt is too much a part of who you are.

It is better to accept when we are neither ready, able, or willing to consider forgiveness at the moment. This is better than pretending to forgive, because you are not fooling anyone, especially not yourself. Pretending to forgive only pushes the anger down deeper and you become a ticking time bomb that can explode at any time. When you are able to forgive, it is an acknowledgement of the hurt done to you, and a recognition of how this hurt and pain has affected your behavior and how you feel. Working on forgiveness allows you to eventually release the power and control that the offending person has over you. You are no longer the victim!

I want to just touch on few ideas on what forgiveness is NOT!!

Forgiving does not mean you condone the offense. As an example, if your partner had an affair, forgiving your partner for the offense does not mean that you condone what he or she did. The affair was wrong, but you do not have to suffer indefinitely because you were betrayed.

Forgiveness does not mean that you must reconcile with someone who treated you badly. For example, if you were abused as a child or were in a harmful relationship, you can forgive the person; as part of that choice, you can also make the decision to end or limit contact. I call this reevaluating the relationship. Forgiveness is for creating your peace of mind. It allows you to heal and be capable of love and trust again. Forgiveness does not have to lead to reconciliation.

Forgiveness does not mean that we forget what has happened to us. Of course, you're going to remember what happened to you. That doesn't mean, that you need to dwell on that hurt or build your life story around the pain.

Painful events can be life-enhancing experiences when we grieve and learn from them. I want you to know that forgiveness is not easy, and it may take some time. It is completely up to you. Take as much time as you need. Pretending to forgive because someone feels you should or tells you that you should is not going to help you. Forgiveness is for you and not for anyone else. You do not even have to tell anyone what you have decided to do. Forgiveness does not mean reconciliation; you have the right to reevaluate and redefine your relationships. We all get to experience life, both the good and the bad. No one is exempt. You have to find peace in the fact that forgiving those who wrong you—even though it is difficult—frees you from holding onto that hurt.

Chapter Five
THE LAW OF ATTRACTION

...

The Law of Attraction is like gravity. You can't see it, but you know it exists.

When I started to think about how to define the Law of Attraction (LOA), I had to sit with it for a moment. There are so many articles and opinions on this subject that for someone new to the concept, it may sound confusing, impossible, or just crazy. So, I decided to give you one more perspective—mine—in the hopes that it makes it simple to understand. There are many people that have the wrong idea of what the LOA is and what it can do for them. Some may think it is some magical way to get what you want by simply thinking positive thoughts. I have mentioned throughout this book that we must take some action to bring things into our reality.

Everything you need to create the life you want already exists inside you. Seek those things out to become the absolute best version of yourself and inspire people around you to be better.

The Law of Attraction is like gravity. You can't see it, but you know it exists. If you are a conscious observer, you can see the LOA in action. If you can learn how to consciously use the Law of Attraction to manifest what you want, you can change your life! It is a process that takes time but can be mastered. You have to be patient and take action. Let me say this again: it is a process, and you must be patient.

Let's look at some concepts that can help with understanding the Law of Attraction.

Vibrations

Everything is a vibration; our brains are so smart that they can take all the vibrations around us and translate them into things that we can recognize, and it becomes our reality. When you think about sound, it is a frequency that vibrates in a way that our brain can translate into something that we can recognize.

I was horrible at being quiet and still. I am always moving, always doing something. I am almost never still. Then one day, I was challenged to go somewhere, anywhere where I could be quiet, listen, and observe the things around me. I found that fascinating things begin to happen when you can practice silence, if only for ten minutes. The first thing that happened to me was I became aware of my emotions, how I was feeling internally and externally. There was a great sense of calm that came over me and an appreciation that I felt for everything I could hear and see. When you are deeply in touch with your own mind and body, you increase your capacity to experience an embodied presence.

Try this activity: Take some time out of your day and sit still and just try to visualize the vibrations of everything around you. Quiet your mind and try to focus and feel all the sounds around you. Just give it a try and see what happens. I think you'll be surprised.

Like Attracts Like

"Like attracts like" in the simplest terms means things with similar energy levels are drawn to each other. They are drawn together based on their vibration. It happens when at least two entities vibrating at the same frequencies are pulled toward each other. So, when you are thinking positive, it can help you attract good things in your life. Unfortunately, the reverse is also true. Negative thoughts can bring you close to negative events in life.

When you can control what you are focusing on, you will be more conscious of what you are attracting to yourself. Your environment plays a big part in influencing your focus, and so do your thoughts, feelings, talk (what you say), and actions. You are drawn to people and things you are in vibrational harmony with, not what you desire or deserve. The vibrational frequency of every living being is influenced by beliefs, thoughts, and feelings. Simply put, with a positive attitude, you can attract positive people, experiences, and events into your life.

According to *The Fundamentals of the Law of Attraction* by Jon Burras, "Thoughts are forms of energy sent ahead and eventually manifest as physical matter. So, the thoughts you think determine the outcome of your worldly experiences, from finances to health, relationships to the environment" (2013). Our thoughts impact every part of our life. We often desire to do marvelous things but become paralyzed by fear, self-doubt, and procrastination. As a result, we become victims of our minds and are stopped in our quests for a better future.

Let me share how I try to think about everything. I try to focus my energy on the positives and shift from being consumed with all the negative stuff. This shift is essential because we attract the things that we focus our energy on. When you put this teaching into practice, and you start seeing all the positive things, **remember that they are and were**

5 » THE LAW OF ATTRACTION

always there; you just lost your ability to see them because you were looking in the wrong direction. You can find positivity by focusing on it. If you're always in a negative state, that's all you're going to see.

Each aspect of your life gravitates toward you through the Law of Attraction. When you fixate on the things that you desire, instead of hindrances that block you from achieving your dreams, you begin to write a new narrative for your life. What type of story of your life do you want to tell? It is no secret that life will be unfair to all of us at times, but how we handle those situations tests our ability to manifest the things we want.

Let me give you a real-life, mundane, run-of-the-mill example. I was talking to a friend about the Law of Attraction, and she told this unremarkable yet pertinent anecdote.

She said, they were looking for tiles for their new house. She'd never thought about tiles in her life before. She had never even given them a second thought because she had always lived in rented houses, and the tiles were just there. So then, suddenly, she needed to decide what tiles she wanted for their new house. So obviously, they started going to tile shops and became quite well-schooled on all things tiling. She realized that when she went to a house, store, hospital, or hotel, she was looking at the floor and the tiles. She was paying attention to them everywhere she went. For example, she was watching something on television. Even though she was deeply involved in the plot, she looked at the tiles in the fictional house on the television and made mental notes about her preferences. It turns out there are some damn pretty tiles out there!

This real-life, ordinary home improvement example is just a silly anecdote that I am sure you can relate to. It's a great example of how when you're focused on something, you will see it everywhere. Bringing this back to the Law of Attraction and positive and negative energy, whatever you're predominantly thinking about is what you're going to start seeing in your life. You will bring it into your life.

The important part is to realize that all the stuff we think we want is already here. We can't see it because we are not looking for it.

Our Thoughts Affect Us Physically

How you are concentrating your energy affects your perception of that area of focus. So, if you're always in a grumpy mood and telling people you are sick, you will begin to focus on illness predominantly. Our thoughts can change our bodies. For example, some women have phantom pregnancies (meaning that their bodies physically change as though they are pregnant even though they are not). They want a baby so badly and focus their energy there so much that, as a result, their bodies change. We have all experienced this powerful connection between our thoughts and body on some level; we think we might have caught the office or work flu, and we believe that any change in body temperature is the beginning of a fever. That alone shows us how powerful our minds are. If you focus on the negative or the positive, you will see some shift or change; it may not be as dramatic as a phantom pregnancy, but if you focus all your energy in one place, look at how it can manifest.

Once, I wanted a new car. So, I saw it on the dealership's website, and I went and drove it. I thought, "Oh my God, this is amazing—I've never seen a car like this before!" And then, of course, similar to my friend and the tiles, I started seeing that car everywhere. Before, it had been invisible to me, and now it was in my psyche; I could see it everywhere.

Of course, this is how advertising works too. Product placements in your favorite TV show will give you a much higher chance of picking out the item in a store. This whole concept is completely eaten up (and not all for good) by the consumer goods companies. Sometimes when

5 » THE LAW OF ATTRACTION

you discuss the Law of Attraction with people, they think it's all a New Age concept. But it is around us all the time and allows us to see what is already there when we focus. You could call it karma, focus, or perspective, but it's by no means new, and we attract things all the time on a subconscious level. I think the Law of Attraction is an incredibly functional tool. Put simply, you're going to attract what you focus on.

Are we responsible for the undesirable things that happen to us? Should we take responsibility for them, or do we think we may be just "unlucky?"

When you are clear and intentional, you will use your thoughts and words to attract what you want.

Every pleasant thing has its unpleasant counterpart. When you focus on an undesirable aspect of something to push it away from you, it only comes closer because you get what you give your attention to whether it is something that you want, positive or negative.

Having a mindset of abundance allows us to attract the things we want. Begin each day on a good note. If you detect you are not feeling well, or your confidence is a little low, look in the mirror and give yourself a pep talk. Transform your mindset from "I think I can" to "I know I can, and I will!" In no time, you will begin to feel better. You deserve to feel good about yourself. Do not starve yourself of the life you desire by choosing to be bound by negativity, anxiety, and what-if scenarios. Instead, deliberately seek out positivity and surround yourself with it so that you can be successful.

When I was younger, I knew people who always seemed to be doing wrong or bad things. But unfortunately, it also looked like they were getting away with those things. As a youngster, if I tried to do something I deemed wrong, I would always get caught. I couldn't understand why. It was so unfair!

I've continued some of the relationships with these people. I've come to find out they're not benefiting from their current or previous wrongdoings after all. They're actually causing more pain in their lives that shows up in different ways. Although it appeared that they were indeed prospering, they were not getting away with anything. Karma may not be a "one-for-one" correlation, but I believe that you will get back whatever you put out there. It's going to show up some way or another. It always does. It may not be tomorrow, it may be a year or decade from now, but it will typically show its face and show up in your life.

The great thing is you can always change. You can constantly shift. Your wrongdoings don't have to be your forever story or journey. One of the best things that we can experience in this life is joy, love, and happiness. Focus on positivity, step out of negativity, and remember that it's never too late to change your perspective for the better.

Chapter Six
GRATITUDE
...

> *"Gratitude is more than an attitude;*
> *it is something that flows out of you".*

- SADHGRU

How Gratitude Helps Attract What You Want

Do you remember the last time you felt truly thankful? Maybe you were thankful for your life, health, people in your life, strength, and your very essence. There are many definitions of what gratitude is or what thankfulness really means. What resonates with me is that gratitude is more than an attitude; it is an all-consuming emotion that just is. It is the quality of being thankful and the readiness to show appreciation and return kindness. When you choose to allow thankfulness to become the state of mind that rules your life, you will lack nothing, and you will be able to see the sunshine in any dark and cloudy situation.

People who live in a steady state of being grateful tend to experience life more abundantly and more intensely in every moment. To express or experience gratitude brings an individual peace of mind and comfort in knowing that things will be fine no matter what. When you feel true gratitude, it starts from within and consumes you. Emotions of love, joy, and thankfulness are so profound that they show externally in different ways. It could be an instant smile on your face, tears that stream from your eyes, or the uncontrollable need to say, "Thank you!" When these emotions show up externally, this is how I know that gratitude is more than an attitude; it is something that flows out of you.

Imagine how it would feel to always be thankful for your life, partner, family, and friends, even in the midst of turmoil. When you are able to feel gratitude even in your hardest moments, it will help to make them a little easier. Most of the time this happens after the experience has passed; you are able to look back at that difficult moment and see where you were then and look at where you are now realizing how far you have come and the strength you had to come through it – and you are grateful. I want to be clear: Gratitude is an expression of appreciation. It is being grateful for all that you have been given, this includes difficult experiences or lessons that we have learned. We experience gratitude when we acknowledge the blessings currently in our lives despite the trials we may face. Expressing gratitude to ourselves helps us reshape our brains and how we subconsciously think about ourselves. Be grateful for you! You may be thankful for your courage and determination or thankful for your health and healing from a physical, emotional, or mental situation. You can find gratitude for being humble in how you handled a difficult conversation, or thankful for the fact that you have a roof over your head.

When you can first be appreciative of yourself, you can easily and mindfully start to have and experience those true feelings of gratitude.

Showing gratitude is also helpful when it comes to building and strengthening relationships. Gratitude is not an emotion that should be taken lightly. It is a subtle power that can transform our lives and the lives of those around us. When we show appreciation to another person it increases the chances that gratitude will be expressed again in the future. Having a genuine feeling of gratitude opens us up to experiencing more goodness in our lives. Showing gratitude to another person can motivate a relationship because it brings about positive thoughts and pleasant emotions.

As humans, we personally hold the power to change our minds and emotions at any time from negative to positive; we can do something about our situations, how we are feeling and what we are thinking. We have a choice. Facing hardships head-on with a heart of gratitude enables us to view the situation differently. When you are in the midst of turmoil, gratitude may *not* be your first reaction, and this is when thankfulness is needed. If you can focus on what you are grateful for, your heart will fill with appreciation, and in this moment, there is less room for anger and hatred.

We must value the people and the things in our lives. Always remain appreciative and show gratitude, then watch how it alters or changes the moment. It will also heighten positive feelings and change your thought process. When we focus on the things in our lives that we are grateful for, we can begin changing how we view life. You cannot feel sadness and gratitude at the same time. By choosing the positive thought over the other, your mind will begin to shift from thoughts of anger, resentment, and lack to thoughts of joy and abundance regardless of what you are experiencing in the moment.

Once you focus and live in gratitude, you start to realize that you lack nothing. Furthermore, you will begin to attract the people, situations, and things that align with you. When you are grateful, this opens up opportunities to receive. Contrary to popular belief, abundance is not having a lot of money or materialistic things. Abundance is taking inventory of our lives, counting our blessings, and focusing on the things that we appreciate in ourselves, in others, and of course, the things that we are blessed with.

6 » GRATITUDE

According to the *Handbook of Positive Psychology* by C.R. Snyder and S. J. Lopez, "Gratitude is a positive, universal characteristic that transcends historical and cultural periods" (2001). They also say that people experience and express gratitude in diverse ways worldwide. In the darkest times of life, gratitude is fundamental because it enables us to begin seeing life through a different lens—a lens of abundance and prosperity rather than scarcity and tragedy. When we are focused and live in gratitude, we may be able to see unpleasant circumstances as an opportunity for growth—being thankful not so much for the circumstance, but rather for the skills that will come from dealing with it. The ability to see the blessings in the face of tragedy is a magnificent human strength. Being grateful for our experiences and hardships is a lesson that teaches us how we can appreciate the good times when they roll in. Don't you feel grateful for Spring after a harsh winter, a gourmet meal or any meal when you have been fasting, and intimacy after a period of abstinence? Appreciation and gratitude must be present together to ensure that an individual's self-worth and personal value are heightened.

As you begin practicing positivity, take a few moments each day to identify what you are grateful for. We often spend time focusing on what we don't have, which tips the scale toward negativity. When you take the time and take a careful look around you, there are so many wonderful things: a beautiful sunset, the bird in a tree, the fun of making your child laugh, being with a lover, or the variety of delicious foods you enjoy. Begin keeping a journal, writing down all the things currently in your life that you are grateful for. Even if you have a bad day, this exercise will remind you of your abundance. It's not necessary to reach for spectacular things. It's much easier to reach for something general, such as a dog that happily greets you at the door, a cup of your favorite tea, or the comfort of your bed.

Through practicing gratitude, you'll gain momentum in expanding your positive experiences. Scientist Robert Emmons tells us that through showing appreciation, one's mood and outlook improve physically and emotionally. Being in a state of gratitude and appreciation enables you to acknowledge the good in your life. Remember that the conscious mind can only have one thought at a time. Negative or toxic thoughts and emotions are blocked when practicing gratitude.

The higher your vibration, the more positive aspects you attract into your life. Take notice of how negative people are always complaining about what they do not have. They never have enough money, they don't like their jobs, and do not have many friends. The latter is probably because their negativity drives people away. When you are grateful, you feel better. That makes you more pleasant and people may want to be around you.

How Do You Express Gratitude?

Saying thank you is much more than just words; it is appreciating the beauty in a sunrise, flowers growing in a field, a cool Spring rain, or a friend that stops by to see how you are. It is not hard to be thankful for the things you have.

If everyone showed gratitude to others, this world would be a much different place. If you helped someone bring groceries to the house, they would smile and say, "Thank you!" You can see gratitude in their expression. It is the same way for everything else. It does not take much—a smile, a thank you, a small gift to someone who went out of their way for you. And when you put out that kind of positive energy, you draw positive energy back to you.

Say a Kind Word

The easiest way to demonstrate gratitude is to say thank you to another person. Saying a few kind words is an effective way to show gratitude. Kind words, spoken from the heart, can heal a troubled soul. Kind words also work for those who are stressed, lonely, or feel unappreciated.

Forgive Someone Who Has Hurt You

When you pardon or forgive someone who has hurt you, what you are essentially doing is lifting a burden from yourself.

Stop to Admire a Beautiful Sight

Taking some time to enjoy the beauty in nature shows appreciation to the universe for the remarkable way that plants grow. From a tiny seed to sprouting leaves to flowering nature—it is a miraculous thing.

Appreciation and Gratitude

While gratitude and appreciation go hand in hand, they are a bit different from each other. Appreciation cannot be regarded as a synonym for the word gratitude. As mentioned, gratitude exists in the state of being thankful. Appreciation, however, is defined as recognition and enjoyment of the good qualities of someone or something. Appreciation is a term that is more recognizable when it comes to valuing a thing or a person. When we value something, we acknowledge its existence and recognize its importance in our lives. One of my favorite quotes by Sarah Ban Breathnach says, "Whatever we are waiting for—peace of mind, contentment, grace . . . it will surely come to us, but only when we are ready to receive it with an open and grateful heart" (1996).

When you deeply appreciate a person or a thing, what type of feeling does that bring? Do you know the feeling of knowing that you are being appreciated? Everyone loves to feel appreciated. With the world continually in turmoil as we try to work every day, maintain relationships and friendships, and search for peace of mind, we must find small things to appreciate and be grateful for.

There are many things that can distract us from positive thinking, love, appreciation, and gratitude in this life. Once you learn to appreciate the smallest things, your days will be more joyful, and your life will be much more pleasurable.

Think back on a time when something traumatic happened in your life. Maybe you were an athlete on a great sports team and got hurt, or perhaps you went to a school where you were treated so poorly that you could not even enjoy the fruits of your labor. How did you respond to the obstacles that you faced? You may have allowed the injury or the heartache to get the best of you. Failed expectations hurt, don't they?

However, focusing on the negative aspects of situations while life continues to move on hurts you even more. When you look back at your life, things were often not as bad as they seemed. You notice that you had loved ones supporting you every step of the way, even when you did not feel it. When you are able to identify the feelings of gratitude and appreciation, you begin to understand how crucial they are for a happy and more fulfilled life. It is the difference between perceiving the world negatively and viewing the world from a more positive standpoint, which turns your life's struggles into triumphs. Learning to appreciate yourself, others, and your experiences—whether good or bad—will enable you to find fulfillment in the darkest times. Where appreciation exists, broken relationships are repaired, productivity is increased, communication is present, and confidence is gained.

Showing appreciation is a choice. When we actively live a life of gratitude and appreciation, it awakens every cell in our bodies. When gratitude and appreciation are shown consistently, they begin to grow in our lives and affect our everyday decisions. Our brains respond to the joy that we bring other people, and in turn, we feel happiness as well.

Gratitude plays a tremendous role in the human experience, especially the emotional aspect. By focusing on gratitude every day, you will enhance your life like never before. Not only will you find joy and pleasure in having an opportunity to transform the energy of the world, but you will also gain satisfaction from the internal feeling that comes with showing gratitude to others.

When we are filled with gratitude, it is easier to see what others have done, and what we appreciate about them. When we do this daily it creates a positive ripple effect of a life full of appreciation and gratitude, rather than one that is consumed with manipulation driven by the feeling of duty and expectation. We are building a lifestyle that can be described as natural, self-sufficient, prosperous, and loving.

When you can develop and maintain a feeling of gratitude, you will be happier. I know you know people who always seem so happy and energetic. They may feel grateful for everything that they have and it shows. When you exhibit feelings of gratitude and show outward appreciation, your life changes and so do the lives of those around you.

As people grow in gratitude, there is a decrease in depression, anxiety, loneliness, and jealousy. Some people even claim that they feel as if they have a better immune system, leading to healthier lives and overall better well-being. People who lead lives of gratitude generally experience more pleasant lives than those who don't.

Gratitude Even in Times of Despair

It is easy to feel gratitude when things are going well. We can celebrate and be happy when someone has a birthday, a new job, a new baby, or graduates. These life events center around gratitude. It is more challenging to be joyful and express gratitude during life's challenging times.

For many people, especially addiction and trauma survivors, feelings of gratitude don't come naturally. When you suffer through grief, illness, addiction, or the loss of a relationship, it can be hard to find anything to be grateful for. When everything around you is crashing down, how do you find something to be thankful for? You have to take it one step at a time. It's easy to let yourself wallow in despair, and it's harder to fight your way out of it.

A popular practice in twelve-step programs is to have the participants write down two things they are thankful for each day. If you can't find anything to be grateful for now, be grateful for waking up today, for friends, for family, clothes, and shelter. When you practice gratitude day after day, it will get more comfortable, and you'll find more things to be grateful for.

Gratitude As a Practice

You may ask yourself, "How can I live a life in constant gratitude?" It is a very thought-provoking question with a reasonably straightforward answer: practice. The more you practice showing gratitude, the easier it will become for you. In little to no time, you'll be living a life full of gratitude and mindfulness.

You can purchase a gratitude journal to help you achieve this goal. A gratitude journal helps you develop a routine of showing constant appreciation, no matter what you are going through. With your gratitude journal, you write down three or more things that you are thankful for each day. These could be things about yourself, other people, or just life in its beauty. Try to collect and remember things, memories, relationships, people, properties, even the little things to be grateful for every day. Also, think about starting good and positive conversations surrounding the topic of gratitude with your peers and loved ones. Hearing other people speak about the things they are grateful for will help you take some time and analyze your own life. You may realize that what you were stressing over was minuscule compared to what someone else has conquered or is currently experiencing. By listening to others, you will become more appreciative of your life, thus creating a feeling of gratitude for life.

Gratitude practices are also very closely linked to positive emotions like joy, peace, and happiness. Once you consciously decide to focus on the positive moments of life and take stock of all the events and things, you're grateful for, you will be able to retrain your brain to make the best of everything and every moment of life.

While being grateful and finding gratitude every day, may sound like an easy thing to do, I will be the first to tell you it is not. The journey will be different for everyone. It takes practice to establish a habit of gratitude.

Transforming our negative thoughts into positive ones and considering all the things we are grateful for can increase our awareness of our lives' blessings. Gratitude is one of the fastest and easiest way to find joy. So, when we are able to practice gratitude we increases the value of our lives and allows us to appreciate others.

Although it gets tough at times, I wake up every day and decide to be mindful of my thoughts and the things I pay attention to. I make it my business to compliment others and point out significant things that may otherwise be overlooked or underappreciated. Additionally, I make sure that I always speak on at least three things that I am grateful for each day and do my best to show myself the utmost love and appreciation.

It is no secret that everyone in this life will experience trials, tribulations, and shortcomings. Have you ever considered using the act of gratitude to shed light on challenging situations? Try practicing these things to help with your transformation:

- Maintain a daily gratitude journal and write out at least three things for which you are grateful.
- Live fully in each moment.
- Practice deep breathing while being still in meditation.
- Quickly switch negative thoughts into positive thoughts by reciting affirmations out loud.
- Tell three people that you love them.
- Pray.
- Learn to appreciate the little things.

There are so many different actions that you can take to live in gratitude. Choose a few to implement into your daily routine and watch how your life changes for the better. Remember that the smallest things sometimes make the most significant difference. What you may think is silly could be the thing that moves you into a mindset of gratitude.

I once read a story about someone who experienced a transforming revelation of gratitude. A woman admired one of her friends in many ways. She was inspired by how he solved problems and how he communicated. She described him with terms like "creative," "amazing," and "brave" but said nothing to him. She thought she had nothing to contribute to him, which caused her to keep her distance. For several years, her unspoken appreciation was an invisible wall between them. Then came a time when she was focused on finding more gratitude in her life, and she got in touch with this man. She wanted him to understand how much she appreciated him and why. He was both relieved and touched. He had noticed that she kept her distance and had interpreted it to mean that she disliked him in some way. At first, she was surprised. Then she realized that, of course, he could not have known how much she appreciated him, because she had never told him anything. After this, he was more human in her eyes, and she finally felt confident that she would be enough in his company.

Being intentional and specific with how we express our appreciation for others affects both their lives and ours. I am sure that many of us have received appreciation that meant the world to us on different occasions. However, do you ever think how someone may feel when you do not express your appreciation? When we do not verbally express ourselves, it leaves room for assumptions and possible disappointments. Expressing gratitude and appreciation for someone should be easy; it Is how you feel. Be free to wholeheartedly communicate your feelings of appreciation and gratitude.

When we show appreciation for others, we relay how a person has made a difference in our lives. If we want to contribute to someone's positive energy, we should start by ensuring that our intentions are clear and free of all motives. Do not show appreciation to entice someone to work harder or guilt-trip someone into doing things for you. Instead, express gratitude when you feel happy and want others to share in your joy. Be clear about why you are expressing appreciation, communicate how an individual has contributed to the betterment of your life, genuinely speak from the heart to let them know how their actions have affected you, and observe their reaction to your appreciation.

Gratitude appears in our lives in a plethora of forms, not just words. Gratitude is much more than merely saying "thank you." It is an enriching feeling that gives us the energy we need to conquer negative emotions like envy, greed, and jealousy. It provides a real sense of freedom. That feeling of freedom allows us to influence the things we want to change and take action.

FINAL THOUGHTS

...

These are the fundamental lessons I have learned that I wish to pass on to you:

- Love yourself
- Forgive
- Be compassionate
- Be grateful
- Be joyful

MOST of all, enjoy this life!

When you incorporate these practices in your life, you will see positive change.

Positive Thinking

Open up to the possibility of positive feelings entering your life. Acknowledge what you're feeling and be OK with it. Positive thinking can change your current state.

Above all remember to be kind to yourself.

FINAL THOUGHTS

Train Your Subconscious Mind

- Limit your exposure to negativity.
- Do not let other people's negative or unexpected opinions set you back. Take care of your dreams and ideas.
- Acknowledge the small achievements.

Vibrations

Vibrational frequencies have a direct correlation to our energy levels. They create our overall vibration of being. Stay at the highest vibration possible.

The Act of Forgiveness

The meaning of forgiveness is important for our spiritual growth. Practice forgiveness every day—forgiving others and forgiving yourself. Accept the things you cannot forgive at this moment, and understand what forgiveness is not.

The Law of Attraction

Remember that like attracts like. When you can shift your thoughts to a more positive mindset, you will attract positive things into your life.

Gratitude

Live a life of constant gratitude and appreciation. Gratitude can change your life. Expressing gratitude for others and appreciating what has been given to us allows us to be open for more good things to come into our lives. Gratitude is a necessary step for practicing positivity.

THIS BOOK FOUND YOU

If you can stay at your highest vibration of love and joy, you will live a magnificent life. It is not always easy, but it can happen with practice. Know that you have choices, and you can choose to love yourself and others. You can always choose better and be grateful for everything that you have. Reclaim your power!

I would love to see you grow and expand with the support that you need on your spiritual journey. If this book has resonated with you in any way and you want to continue your journey with me as your coach, you can find me at Quiet-Counsel.org.

Love and Light

ACKNOWLEDGE-MENTS

...

First and foremost, I want to give thanks and praise to my creator. This book was made possible by meeting people with whom I shared values and working alongside them on my journey.

It is so important to surround yourself with people who are like-minded, who support you in many ways, and who are truly selfless and want only the best for you. I want to acknowledge the people who have helped me and continue to support me on my journey.

Mrs. Deborah Foggio, the owner and founder of LightWorks Enterprises, was, and is, instrumental in guiding me, mentoring me, and helping me find my true purpose.

Claire Robbin has helped me to write this book. Working with Claire has been amazing. She is gifted and talented, and I am proud to think of her as a friend.

I have been truly inspired by so many, from family and friends to other coaches and spiritual leaders in the community. I am grateful and appreciative. Thank you!

REFERENCES

...

"Fundamentals of the Law of Attraction," Ascension Now, accessed October 16, 2020, http://www.ascensionnow.co.uk/the-law-of-attraction.html.

"How to Reprogram Your Subconscious Mind," Medium, accessed, July 22, 2020 https://medium.com/change-your-mind/reprogramming-your-subconscious-mind-ecaae9640aad (article removed).

"The Power of Positive Thinking," Johns Hopkins Medicine, accessed February 19, 2021, https://www.hopkinsmedicine.org/health/wellness-and-prevention/the-power-of-positive-thinking.

"The Power of Your Subconscious Mind," Farnam Street, accessed, December 6, 2021, tps://fs.blog/2017/03/power-subconscious-mind/.

"What Is Positive Mindset: 89 Ways to Achieve a Positive Mental Attitude." 2018. PositivePsychology.Com. July 5, 2018. https://positivepsychology.com/positive-mindset/.

Baggott, Jim. Quantum Theory: "If a Tree Falls in the Forest. . ." OUPblog, accessed February 16, 2021, https://blog.oup.com/2011/02/quantum/.

Burras, Jon. "The Fundamentals of the Law of Attraction," The Inside of You, accessed October 18, 2020, https://www.truthinsideofyou.org/the-fundamentals-of-the-law-of-attraction/.

Carter, Zack. "Freedom in Forgiveness," Psychology Today, accessed October 16, 2020, https://www.psychologytoday.com/us/blog/clear-communication/201706/freedom-in-forgiveness.

REFERENCES

Cherry, Kendra. "What Is Positive Thinking?" Very well Mind, accessed October 15, 2020, https://www.verywellmind.com/what-is-positive-thinking-2794772.

Dobbins, R. D "The Healing Power of Forgiveness," Pentecostal Evangel, accessed August 7, 2020.

Edberg, Henrik. "12 Powerful Tips to Overcome Negative Thoughts (and Embrace Positive Thinking)," The Positivity Blog, accessed October 5, 2020, https://www.positivityblog.com/overcome-negative-thoughts/.

Elkins, Chris. "What Is a Higher Power?" DrugRehab.com, accessed May 18, 2021, https://www.drugrehab.com/recovery/faith-and-religion/what-is-a-higher-power/.

Emmons, Robert. "Why Gratitude Is Good," Greater Good Magazine, accessed October 11, 2021, https://greatergood.berkeley.edu/article/item/why_gratitude_is_good/.

Emmons, Robert A., and Michael E. McCullough. "Counting Blessings Versus Burdens: An Experimental Investigation of Gratitude and Subjective Well-Being in Daily Life." *Journal of Personality and Social Psychology* 84 no. 2 (2003): 377–389. https://whish.stanford.edu/wp-content/uploads/2018/11/GratitudeArticle.pdf.

Fredrickson, Barbara. 2009. *Positivity*. Harmony.

Fredrickson, Barbara L, Michael A. Cohn, Kimberly A. Coffey, Jolynn Pek, and Sandra M. Finkel. "Open Hearts Build Lives: Positive Emotions, Induced Through Loving-Kindness Meditation, Build Consequential Personal Resources." *Journal of Personality and Social Psychology* 95, no. 5, (2008): 1045–1062, https://doi:10.1037/a0013262

Goldbleck, Madison. "15 Things to Know About a Spiritual Awakening UWM Post, accessed January 17, 2021, https://uwmpost.com/featured-columns/15-things-know-spiritual-awakening.

Hicks, Esther, and Jerry Hicks. 2005. *Ask & It Is Given*. Carlsbad, CA: Hay House.

Hicks, Esther, and Jerry Hicks. 2004. *Ask and It Is given: Learning to Manifest Your Desires*. Carlsbad, CA: Hay House.

"Spiritual How to – Learn Spirituality – Spiritual Information – Spiritual Life." n.d. Spiritualhowto.Com. Accessed April 26, 2021. http://spiritualhowto.com.

McGreevey, Sue. 2011. "Eight Weeks to a Better Brain." Harvard Gazette. January 21, 2011, accessed, May 19, 2021. https://news.harvard.edu/gazette/story/2011/01/eight-weeks-to-a-better-brain/.

Mullins, Eddie. "The Process of the Law of Attraction and the 3rd Law, Law of Allowing." Unpublished master's thesis, University of Wisconsin-Stout, 2008. http://www2.uwstout.edu/content/lib/thesis/2008/2008mullinse.pdf

Nevid, Jeffrey S. "Is Your Brain on Automatic Pilot? Isn't It Time to Take Control?" Psychology Today, accessed, October 12, 2020 https://www.psychologytoday.com/us/blog/the-minute-therapist/201803/is-your-brain-automatic-pilot.

Robert, Emmons A. "The Psychology of Gratitude," (PDF) EPDF, accessed October 18, 2020, https://epdf.pub/the-psychology-of-gratitude-series-in-affective-science.html.

Snyder, C. R., and Shane J. Lopez, eds. 2012. *Handbook of Positive Psychology*. New York, NY: Oxford University Press.

Stinson, Annakeara. "How to Control Your Thoughts During Meditation, According to Experts," Elite Daily, accessed October 16, 2020, https://www.elitedaily.com/p/how-to-control-your-thoughts-during-meditation-according-to-experts-8993641.

Wiest, Brianna. "13 Ways to Start Training Your Subconscious Mind to Get What You Want," Forbes, accessed July 20, 2021, https://www.forbes.com/sites/briannawiest/2018/09/12/13-ways-to-start-training-your-subconscious-mind-to-get-what-you-want/#78ad2f067d69.